Emotional Traffic

Emotional Traffic

POEMS BY

Ira Sadoff

DAVID R. GODINE · PUBLISHER

Boston

For Dianne and Dennis
who helped see me through

First edition published in 1989 by
David R. Godine, Publisher, Inc.
Horticultural Hall
300 Massachusetts Avenue
Boston, Massachusetts 02115

Library of Congress Cataloging-in-Publication Data

Sadoff, Ira.
  Emotional traffic.
  I. Title.
PS3569.A26E46   1989   811'.54   88-45807
ISBN 0-87923-782-1 SC

First edition
Printed in the United States of America

The author wishes to thank the following magazines for printing earlier versions of the following poems:

The American Poetry Review: "Dursu Uzala," "The Bath"; *Antæus*: "The Way of All Flesh," "Zinfandel," "Incest"; *Chelsea*: "Central Avenue Breakdown"; *The Carolina Quarterly*: "Mingus: Last Speech"; *Crazy Horse*: "At the Half Note Cafe," "Why It's Impossible to Cross the Same Ocean Twice," "Sunrise: Two Artichokes and an Onion"; *The Missouri Review*: "The Pink Gardenia"; *The New England Review/Bread Loaf Quarterly*: "Honduras," "Nazis," "Notre Dame (1909)"; *The New Republic*: "At the Jazz Concert"; *The New Yorker*: "A Northern Calendar" (originally published as "Gathering Kindling"), "January: First Light"; *The Paris Review*: "Pemaquid Point"; *The Partisan Review*: "Walking Down Castro Street After Frank O'Hara"; *Ploughshares*: "Blue Lights," "Intimacy at First Light: Bath, Maine, Shipyard," "North Platte: August, 1968," "Summer Solstice in Praise of the Bourgeois," "The Vacation in Miami: July, 1954," "Why We Always Take Vacations by the Water"; *Poetry*: "Bleak House," "Checks and Balances: Oakland, Maine," "My Wife's Upstairs"; *Sewanee Review*: "Now"; *Shenandoah*: "Memorial Days"; *Three Rivers Journal*: "August," "Ode to Experience"; *The Yale Review*: "After a Disappointing Visit With Old Friends I Try in Vain to Recover the Joys of Childhood," "In the House of the Child."

"Nazis" was reprinted in the 1985 *Anthology of American Verse*, Monitor Press. "After a Disappointing Visit With Old Friends I Try in Vain to Recover the Joys of Childhood" was reprinted in the 1984 *Anthology of American Verse*, Monitor Press.

The following poems also appeared in the chapbook *A Northern Calendar*, David R. Godine, Publisher: "January: First Light," "Bleak House," "Dursu Uzala," "Intimacy at First Light : Bath, Maine, Shipyard," "Pemaquid Point," "Summer Solstice in Praise of the Bourgeois," and "Walking Down Castro Street After Frank O'Hara."

The following poems have been included in *The Bread Loaf Anthology of Contemporary Poetry*: "Memorial Days," "Mood Indigo," "Nazis," "Why We Always Take Vacations By the Water."

The author would like to thank the National Endowment for the Arts for awarding a Creative Arts Fellowship to help complete work on this book.

*

Contents

Emotional Traffic

I.

_____

"All things are tragic
When a mother watches!"

—Frank O'Hara
Poem

In the House of the Child

If you hear the chatter of water
beneath the ice-capped stream, if you hear
the creaking oak lightning took away,

it's because nothing's been discarded here,
though the cabinets have been emptied out,
and the closet's scent is purely cedar.

Long after a son's renounced his mother's dream
of him, long after he's settled in the city
with her duplicate or opposite, he comes back

to mother her, to memorize a sight, to clear a place.
Spoons click in their tray. The table must be set.
A candle's lit for dinner. The trail of light

from then to now is snow the storm
condenses on the windowsill. The house
remembered gives no shelter from the winter.

But it seems to me there's too much light
at four A.M. Too much frost. Too much of her
when her nightgown with its crown of lace

flutters on the frozen clothesline,
when furniture's shifted from the fireplace
to suggest sufficient warmth and space.

I never think of her.
Never, or almost never, and always when
I first wake up, when the bedroom door's ajar.

The Ballad of the Favorite Son

Like those who compose in Spanish,
he is in love with regret.

Something about the composition of oranges
or a sunlit balcony
brings to his tongue the words *before* or *after*.

His mother, who will not go to heaven
because of a ballet slipper,

what does she remember of the row houses,
the dog's chalky tongue,
the promised loaf of bread, more than bread?

She preferred to dance, though he never saw her dance.
It's a long story, a love affair on stage

she savored, though it went on for hours, not for years.
The boy was shaky on his own,
a coin dropped from a pocket onto cobblestones.

Oh but she spent her days with him in the meadow
watching over him. Gazing over him,

with a tearful, sentimental eye toward the afternoon sun,
magenta and pink. In his absence,
she peeled an orange for her son. And held it up to him.

The Bath

1.

Mother might have drowned me,
had she caught me watching her.
I watched her scrub her skin so hard
it seemed to blush. I saw desire there,
before a mother wants to be a mother.
The keyhole—ring of light that skims the flesh—
drew me to the pleasure. I understood
the glistening surface of the belly, the bumpy
shadows of the ribcoast range. I understood
that water scalds, dripping from the wrist.
Everything else, like a lamp
turned on and off, was thought: pure, impure, pure.

2.

Years later, I can't repair the shock of hair
crackling to the static of her brush,
or grant her mermaid's wishes. I can't
re-trace her hands: the first amphibians
waiting to emerge. In the beginning
we know too much of everyone
until we fail them, until we see them
as they can't be seen. When Actæon
came upon Diana's naked body
and the dogs made cloth of his flesh,
he knew he'd truly burn. His voice
was not his own, his face not his face.
How could one touch heal all of us?

3.

Since I can't go back
to what I wanted, since the flesh
refuses its own flesh, I can't suggest
what might have pleased them,
those long-haired creatures whose touch
soothed and satisfied. What pleases them,
these mothers, sisters, lovers,
whose oars row out to the island
I keep lonely? What pleased her
she never said. That night I saw her dream
so sheer, so self-contained, that mist surrounded it.
I never knew its subject matter.
The flesh has its cannibals, its boiling pots.
We prepare the body badly for its future.
Every household is full of crimes.
A moon shines in every window, wanting.
Each night I hold a different woman in my arms.

The Vacation in Miami: July, 1954

In his yellow swimsuit, in the heat of July,
they sent him to his room, the suggestion

of his father's hand. It was the shape
of a passing cloud—the burnished palm

left a taste in his mouth: charcoal.
A moment not worth remembering.

But the hotel and its ammonia smell, palm
trees bristling, seemed an invitation

to the ocean. He watched couples approach
the water cautiously, and grownups

protected by umbrellas from the acid heat.
The room, the white stucco walls, cut him off

from his small friends, the way a rubber band
breaks the circulation on a wrist. Blue.

The children whispered to each other
his punishment. He knew what they thought.

What was his crime? He could not quite remember.
It had something to do with swimming out too far,

with firecrackers that fell from his pocket
while wrestling his father on the grass.

Exile seems too strong a word, and reminds him
of his father smoking cigarettes, waving

to strange women in their bathing suits,
following one to her room. But left alone

the boy swam out, caught his father's guilty slap.
And watched the Fourth of July from his window:

the darkened ocean reflecting evening sky,
his parents' argument, the fireworks' bright display.

Why We Always Take
Vacations by the Water

For too long I've watched the ski boat scan
the water the way a gull might pan for fish.
What's a ski boat? I don't know
exactly, and I've never heard of one
discussed on those dogged New England wharfs.

But the boat has spindly legs
which keeps its frame from touching ocean
like a reluctant swimmer: my mother
on vacation. What was she doing there
by herself while men read at pool side?

My father must have been long gone, writing
the signs of his legible desire: one love letter
after the next. All his girlfriends, I think,
were waiting to have something written
on their faces: waves and lines and furrows,

scrutable maps of where they'd been.
The body had already taken its toll
on my mother—even then I remember wanting
some middle-aged man to appreciate her
the way I did, only more so. I don't love her

that way, though I still have feelings I can't name.
Did I talk about the noise it makes, the boat
with "foils," "ailerons," the puttering machine
like a nagging voice in a cinder block motel?
I often wonder why he left. Too often. Why my wife

and I fight over where to take our one week off
every year and we're still here. None of us can swim.
That's a helpless feeling, like speaking for your parents
when they were far from here twenty years ago.
How did I get from there to here? My confusion

brought me, a silly vehicle I've never seen before
that caught my eye, and a handsome man
in a yachting cap waving from its stern—
he's saying something to my mother we can't hear
as she lets her body slip into the ocean, almost bare.

She doesn't wear a bathing cap, my father notices
her hair spreads on the surface of the water
like a skirt blown upward in a sudden wind.
It maddens us, the passage from a swimming pool
to an unknown boat, a stranger at the helm.

Mood Indigo

I've tried to trace the reverie
without a source. Why I love
that shade of blue the veins become
when you press a thumb against my wrist.
Why I take the bunting weighing down
the branch of pine as a sign
it's lost, searching for its mate.
Why I think of nineteen forty-four,
the argument before my birth:
it should have warned my mother
how the future held her
like the violent blue of storm.
Like a tablet dropped into a glass
of water, this mood dissolves
and bubbles up a murky brew
of hurt and anger misconstrued.
The color of a bruise, a child
before he draws his first traumatic breath.
Why put a stop to it? Because the hook
of waking in the dark
drags me toward the morning light,
because I must consume the cold sublime,
the bowl of plums that calls us to the table.

Incest

Inbred. Inscribed. Interred. In my house,
the doors locked, the lips
stuck to each other (like glue, she said), languishing—
each seduction is a slash,
an utterance with body parts, a slang
of neck submerged in whispers. What breast belongs to a mother
exclusively? What speech does not imply
withholding union, the little boy
having sex with his past? I'm not stirred
by strangers. Each taboo's a story
ending, bones a dog buried in the yard,
the neatly-pressed negligee set out on the bed.
Someone drew the shades, the eyelids closed,
her finger on his lips
authored in the hush. Kiss me goodbye,
she said. Her flesh
an entrance without exit. Shame's
the world's. It's not myself
I hate.

August

Under the yellow porch-light,
a few moments before sunrise,
I still hold her close to me,
as if to move the face beyond deciphering.
A few moments before Mother appears
in the housecoat I want no one to see.
She's all throat. Her voice is sultry,
hurt, full of indirection.

I stand there, petrified,
with the woman whose cheek I remember
as red, hot to the touch, steamy
as the air inside our greenhouse in August.

I circle the event on my old calendar
because thirty years of rage
is too hot to hold. I won't forget
my burning wrist, the scalding coffee cup,
before she rubs the invisible salve
into the wound. Now she wakes
too close to me, a hundred miles away.
Her vigil is a passage I walk through.
On the other side of the kitchen door
trumpet vines are climbing the trellis,
and just beyond the picket fence, in a summer dress,
the woman I want to marry circles the yard.

In the Mountains

I see the woods as threads.
I dread being lost in them, unraveling.
I've been wandering all night, trying to find
a state where I can rest. I think of Trakl,
staggering in the woods, drunk, disconsolate,
dispossessed. He loved his sister from a distance,
as if he saw her sideways in the mirror.
The words are threads; I wish the leaves
could scan the pines for paths. Trakl saw bats
where there were none. Blue light
when he himself was blue. His sister
wore a necklace which made her approachable.
Those beads were wound together, like a family.
Like a family of words, I am watching him
when I am lost, watching out for him
when he's already dead.
The woods are lost when I'm watching them.
The stands of pine, the shadow the moon makes of them.
My sister in the woods on a starry night. Half-paralyzed
in her car. Her slender body bent like poplar.
In my dream I'm looking for the doctor.
The woods are threats. I'm far from her,
my sister, my specter, whose voice is splintered, glass.

Memorial Days

for Robert and Yvette Sadoff

Whirlwind with a vacuum at four A.M.,
Mother always closed the blinds
so neighbors never knew her business.
I never knew what occupied
that frenzied mind: she kept the house so clean
and dark, streaks of morning light
seemed obtrusive as a visit from my father.

She called me *Robert* in his absence,
though the word I thought I heard meant *thief*.
I never figured what I stole from her
but rest. I'd wake her from my nightmare
until she'd soothe me back to sleep
with a washcloth and a kiss. Near dawn,
dissheveled, drained, short of breath,

she'd dissolve an aspirin on her tongue,
and on our couch collapse. But not before
she rubbed the mirrors clear, dispersed the dust
off old photographs. Her bronze ballet slippers
waxed brightly in the light, or was it dusk
before her rags wiped clean those memories?
No complaints, she'd say, or *Keep them to yourself.*

She acted hers out like a mime. Long after
she stretched before a full-length mirror
and spun her pirouettes toward the future,
her accompanist, my father. Where was he
on this holiday? She said simply, *Men,*
they can't be counted on. It was Monday
and I didn't have to leave for school.

I thought I heard my mother's heart
beating like a bat beneath an eave. Covered by a sheet
she scared me into thinking she was dead.
My hand startled her awake. She called me
by my father's name, on a day I can't forget.
Memorial Day. The day we're called on
to recall the living and the living dead.

Blue Lights

I was seven. I took the train to Ossining.
Blue lights, a symphony domestica, families fastened in
across the river from the prison. The air smelled of laundry.
At the hospital: coughing, a swinging light bulb,
a few inarticulate phrases. In another century
I might have prayed. Did I understand, he asked,
what it meant to live without hope for the future?
Disease is a film over the eye, a drawn shade
above the heart, and where we're most private
it strikes. Steam from the locomotive is still
the air I breathe and the greasy windows
coming home give witness to the passing world.
Uncle, I say. Uncle. A sullen kind of surrender,
the haze of language. Breathtaking clouds.

Why It's Impossible to Cross
the Same Ocean Twice

I lived, as a child, near the ocean
where my family fought on our pleasure boat.
Nudged past breakers and swells, we floated out
on sunny days, dazed into helplessness.
I liked it. If I drifted into hurt—
into "suffering" seems too strong a word—
and steered us toward some shallow danger
on the rocks, I gave my parents' lectures
little thought. Like God's word, Father's shouts
and pointless directions, Mother's fears
of water, were givens: if you wanted sunlight
on the ocean's surface, hysteria became your partner.
By dusk we anchored, tired of strife, hungry
for a little privacy. Those nights I slept in peace.
I remember a Sunday when a gull crossed our path
and struck our hull. It floated, eyes
open, for a moment stunned,
expressionless, then lashed out its clumsy wings. Later,
the bird swooped down, caught the fish it wanted.
There was no moral in it. Only in reflection
when I look into these same waters
and see some distortion of a childish face
I invented, can I call up the bruises
my parents might have caused. I survive them now.
And I understand why an eyelid is required
to protect the eye, not so much from injury
as from seeing too much, from taking the truth
too seriously. The sea is not so personal.

Emotional Traffic

A pretty woman in a cape passes by my window.
I like watching her now instead of worrying.
She's lifted from some famous painting

by Bonnard, where fruits and breads, bright spheres of light,
yellows, browns and reds, decorate the kitchen table.
Everybody's happy. She's stolen a boy's diary

because she has to know what's in someone else's mind.
I like to think I'm in my undershirt, my mind's
a vat of beaujolais. A dreamer, no longer

driven, I have someone else's parents. All the balloons
in town are filled with gravel, and floating upward,
ascension, as they used to call it,

is frowned upon. So I'm down in the dumps, trying to describe
what fills the window. The familiar's so familiar
I don't want to tell you how blue is blue,

how I'm like my mother. The giant blue jays in the oak should be
waxwings. I'd like my childhood not to weigh
a thousand pounds. A woman in a cape

passed by my window. She talks all day—it takes all day
to make the beds. Since there's no telephone
she talks to herself. She complains

about her husband, that old sack of flour. She wants
her son under foot, so he can use the broom.
Each word makes her less mysterious,

more my mother. The road that once led to the village
where neighbors live, where bakers mix up flour
with politics, where the public's not private,

still takes me home again, to the same old field of light
that colors what I see. I must weed out passages
that refer just to me. So the woman

in the cape can rest more easily. The book's her window to
the world: she must find the torn out pages baffling:
but she can guess I'm bored to death with her.

January: First Light

I retrace the path
of the old railroad tracks
just before light. No noise:
the barn owl drifting into sleep,
the birds not yet awake.
The iron scars
have been melted down
for a war long fought and gone.
Then the evening edged out
by the first band of light,
across the strips of trees.
I know
I don't have long to go:
the sleepless night that brought me
to the woods behind the house
is over now, and what fears I had
I left behind me there.
In the distance I make out rabbit tracks
and behind them, something larger,
a dog perhaps, on its trail.
The trail leads nowhere
and the rabbit's safe.
A world without predators: the parent's
dream. Why won't it pass?
Look: the starling's pulled that ribbon
of worm, the day's unraveling,
we're moving on, exhausted, ready to begin.

II.

"Good Morning Blues. Blues how do you do?
Blues say, 'I feel all right but I come to worry you.'"

—Jimmy Rushing
"Good Morning Blues"

Sunrise: Two Artichokes and an Onion

This is for those who flower
to bitterness. For the flowers of abundance,
of too many petals: the green thorn-flower,
the flower scraped clean, whose buttery
heart must be eaten through.
                              And its cousin
of so many layers, so often circled,
cast off, misunderstood. So it opens to emptiness:
those who know loss know that gesture
of giving, the pause between darkness
and first half-penny of sun.

It's morning now: the checkered clouds
rise over the hillside, blue and white
fields too distant, like a wish, to be touched.
To be consumed, to disappear, this is the desire
of those unloved, the red and green, the first light
we shy away from, those we want to flower for.

Dursu Uzala

---

after Kurosawa

Morning. The plane rises,
tilts from side to side. My insides
slightly raw, for no reason.

In the theater, the strained
images of Kurosawa come back
to me unchanged: sunrise in the taiga,
swamp grass bending, the long journey

of those who can't adapt: we touched,
secretly, as if ashamed by lust. We had our lives,
those we belonged to, and would not
give them up. To disappear and be far

from others isn't what we desire, it's
our escape. Sleeping by myself is barbarous,
so is sleeping with someone else.

Now, the tiny houses almost breathing,
the unmarked roads, snow blowing past
their borders, free and hardly visible . . .

What is it I ask from you,
from anyone? The connection between strangers
is easy if intimate, barren
as a land explored but never farmed.

A tiger appeared in that forest,
so beautiful a savage it seemed
almost tame. But we grew closer
to its hunger, were taken back

by our fears. I don't want to go home,
and I can't stand a single place.
Your touch will be remembered, the wish
for friendship, which, in flight

might take us home but will not hold.

My Wife's Upstairs

My wife's upstairs,
hard at work.
I don't understand
what she thinks about
in that tiny room
looking out at the apple trees,
an ordinary field, a thread of stream.
She's thinking of something else.

It's a dreary day, though the foliage
makes its first appearance
on the locust trees, bales of hay
stacked neatly by the farmer's barn.
She's thinking of something else.
Surrounded by books, strands of hair
I imagine in her eyes, a gaze
she offers the window, a distance all her own.

Those books are long journeys,
train rides through the Urals,
parlors in which lovers meet
but can't openly speak. In the next room,
parents, the police, a nosy concierge.
Several kinds of intrigue.
She's so quiet as to be invisible.

I put my ear to the door,
every sense alert. So close
I can almost feel her pulse and breath.
But my wife's far away in that room,
out of the ordinary, fills that space
with longing, the aroma of fallen apples,
the space a single room can't hold.

A Northern Calendar

I pick up the fallen branches,
receive pleasure from their rising
stack on our front porch. We're short
of wood this year, but little else.
Like time for our affections,
though we hardly speak of them.

The ash tree seems to suffer less
its loss; its name assumes
its purpose then: to burn and yet
return to bloom. I can't decide
how we're alike or not in what we need,
though we're joined longer than we remember,

and most others. In the wedding photos
we're drunk with pleasure and a little fear.
We suspected the future, etched in our faces,
would not be known. Where we were born
trees were small enough to step on, few enough
to count. We've arrived at a different place.

The November countryside's not pastoral,
nor is it barren yet. The grass—shades
of brown and green—the leafless trees
sway and breathe with wind. So we gather
by the wood stove, warm our hands on logs
I started up with twigs. I'm a little too proud

of them and us, and not sure enough our store
will keep us from those storms Maine winters bring.

Pemaquid Point

The lighthouse as an image
of loneliness has its limits.

For as we stand on the shore
of this ocean, the crusted snow

on the granite hills and grass
disguised beneath it, that tower

seems a place where people gather
some vision of themselves: the marriage

of rock to water, of wave to snail
washed up on shore. We're small,

and waving to the lobster boat—
which could be miles away or close

enough to raise our voices to—makes
us wish our journeys took us further,

past witness, to a scene where
we belonged. A man in blue

pulls up his net: tiny fish
swim free of it. And the man

pulling anchor, whose strength
tugs him farther from the shore,

pays tribute to our rootlessness.
As he shouts to start the engine up,

to take his course, he leaves us
in the distance, the repeated ritual

of his wake. And like the water
stirred against the lighthouse wall,

breaking up, wave after wave, we
forget ourselves. Learn our place.

Half-Moon Bay

We came to watch the gray whales spawn.
But the ocean turned to fog, miles of it,
and yards from shore no water could be seen.
To make the most of it, we climbed the rocks
and listened to the building storm.

Our breath, so visible, reminded me
of flukes, the rise and fall of love. Years ago,
propelled by hope, we might have turned toward home
and raged all afternoon. I mean to say
I shared your sudden burst of grief

when a couple passed us with their crying child.
We've walked for years that crest of yes and no,
the child as burden, child as cure.
I'm tired of the future, the relentless tide
that pulls us from the ridge of happiness.

Here and now, from the site where some are born,
I want to praise the ocean scent, the half-full moon.

Summer Solstice
in Praise of the Bourgeois

A few humbling things.
Outside my real house
there's an actual picket fence,
a flower box, one shady maple,
and a lawn too big to mow.
I said I'd never come to this.

I said a lot of things.
And sulked, tempestuous, as seasons
passed, unworthy of fierce attention.
My greatest fear: fathers grew fat
and dull, swayed and fell, weighed down
by small concessions to the ordinary.

So today's a kind of turning point.
First the days grew long,
now I can't keep up. I'm left
with evenings, less of them, and a little light.

Tonight's excitement? A walk
around the block, counting inchworms
dangling from the pines.
Watching neighbors clear their dishes,
someone's grandpa tinker in his garage.
I wish I had a daughter to show them to.

This morning in the glare of sun
that shaped my vision of the road, I sped
past a hitchhiker, his life possessions
light enough to lie beside him
in a ditch. His sad face told a story
I knew too well. That's why I left him there.

And praised this day for standing still.

Intimacy at First Light:
Bath, Maine, Shipyard

1.

Not to speak when we're so close
is to be small and shapeless, unlike the other,
small and not part of the clouds, the islands
of sky, the inhaled breath. To forget
women while gazing at their form.

The navies are formless, ships without number,
planted in the ocean as on plateaus or vales.
But peace in the countryside is speechless
and without form: the way you can't count sheep
in that meadow, the way footsteps disappear

on frozen ground. At the beginning of daylight
the last flaking star, the flaking star
of evening, falls and grows dark in the hills
without shadow, falls without will,
loses its pulse and impulse, its crystal shape.

2.

The knowledge of her was like knowing
each day, familiar and so unknown.
She was without figure and a presence
that drew his attention: to think of her
was to invent her form over and over.

3.

The dull film of being, which we cannot see
or take in, but understand; the fission
of daylight, the colorless flesh that takes shape
in every mooning over someone else, in everyone
we wish to bring close by act or speech,

there lies the delight, the coldest spring
drifting and wandering into oceans,
the unseen anchor that makes ships seem
so still. So even without a word or breeze
we might move close and hold the bulk

of us as we pass from birth to death,
and take hold of what tatters and falls,
the tiny flag on the ship's mast, the signal
that stands without decoding, our shapes
as they remember us, the dissembling clouds.

The Way of All Flesh

All those sultry kisses,
addressed, like a waving hand
to the sinking ship, Titanic,
must not go to waste. Save
the kerchiefs and the ticket stubs,
those wishes, lost, for last good-byes.
All those foghorns, pulled-up
anchors, ghostly loves,
and metabolic rushes
add up to a corpse whose body's
given back to him, briefly,
like a miracle. So you rise
from the coffin of the single bed,
full of fresh ideas and plans
to beat the system, to meet your wife
halfway between the kitchen
and the steamy corridor. The body
travels. So those post cards
from Nape Neck and Cheekbone,
from Pelvis and Wrist,
remind you of the summer romance
that lasted till October. And here,
in middle age, where passengers
have packed their recollections
for the final drowning, one wish
might stand for all of us: the porthole
opens on a turgid, salty, autumn sea:

your friend, Lucille, whose thigh
you once spent all night nibbling,
comes back wanting, in her rowboat
full of greed, far more. *Amour,*
she says, *I'm lost,* and lingers
in your memory like the spray
before the breaking wave.

After Dreaming

My kitchen's steamier than Eden,
and the window's just a wishing well.

The eyelids seem to whisper: *gaze,* then *glaze.*
It's time to shut the senses down

the way the rich must bar the shutters
of their summer houses each September.

For now, my cup's a ledge
that begs for my attention. Whoever calls

the children home must have known my mother.
Whoever huddles in the bushes must have known

who stammered there. I can almost see who shakes
the tree, and hear his sudden fall from grace.

The valley and the well, the fault the earthquake
seizes, they provide a home, private and familiar.

The world's so small. I want to push myself aside.
The lip of the cup's no lip to kiss.

From a Myth

The asters are tenacious.

I know what it means to love someone.
Whole fields of them.
To hurt them, as if with a scythe.

When I keep her a body, I do nothing but stare.

Once I let myself wander
through the meadow
to set my sights and to appraise.

One can be common and crushed. Kept in a vase.

If they were friendly, they'd be daisies,
violet and blue. Violent only when unbuttoned.
When the night has a fever, it cries in the morning.

Cobwebs on the grass, a sure sign of frost.

Perhaps it was me. Perhaps it was me
who left an impression, a scar on the grass.
I still walk around it, closing my eyes.

If I keep her a body, I won't have to watch her.

Wincing, should she call me back, to forgive.
The unforgivable eye: a sure sign of frost.
The mind has its reasons

for wishing petals were spokes on a wheel.

I turned away. As if she turned me away.
The meadow means nothing
when you touch someone once.

In the meadow, my footsteps.

Walking Down Castro Street
After Frank O'Hara

The streets of San Francisco
go on too long
which is a pleasant thing
like "going out of our way"
when we're just out walking
without a destination in mind

I'm in one of those moods
when I'm ready for anything
walking without purpose or compulsion
which doesn't mean you're not compelling
but I have to pay attention to the arguments
in the gay bars and pasta stores
the tourists with cameras and colorful road maps
and musicians whistling Fats Waller tunes
and dancing on the sidewalks

Who knows where all this will lead
is it the movie where Frank O'Hara suddenly appears
as a figure in a Larry Rivers painting
just because he might have observed these details
so casually they'd all come together
in a loving assessment of the avenue
with the couples who love and hate one another
some of whom seem lost without their French roast coffee
and others who don't know where they're going
and are in no real hurry to arrive

The Pink Gardenia

Almost forty, and just today
I saw my first pink gardenia
in the back yard of my neighbor.
How much time I've wasted
half-sleeping through my chores—
clipping bushes, stalking weeds—
when I should have dreamed this up
just by looking. Shouldered by
the prickly pear and a palm
full of hummingbirds, the flower
seemed on show, a museum
piece, part of a movie set
from Tahiti. The oval petals,
as if just waxed, caught a drop
of dew for me or anyone
who paid attention.
I've never seen that shade
of pink before, except
on my first love, the blush.
The fragrance was a cup
of tea, a robe of silk
with my favorite body in it.
I watched this bloom for hours
till the petals folded up;
and then, at home, thumbing
through my guide to flowers,
I guess I got the genus wrong:
I know it wasn't white or yellow,
the one exotic, nameless flower
that brought me to my senses.

Now

Now that I'm past my prime,
past the time when Byron, Keats, and Poe
said their eloquent good-byes,
now that I know I'll never play the cello,
that my earnest signature
won't save the world from nuclear war,
now that my middle-aged body
lives in the same hotel as the adolescent
who bangs on the radiator to complain about the heat,

even though I miss the roller coaster rides with Wanda,
even though I want my old love letters back
to admire my handiwork and my sincerity,

I'm ready for the afternoon snow,
the way it rests on the birches
like epaulets on the lieutenant's shoulder
in the Tolstoi novel I've been reading.
I'm prepared to consider injustice
from the wing chair as well as the picket line,
I can accept your invitation to the present
the way the Duke of Windsor
might accept an invitation to the prom,
the way Anna Karenina, wakened from the nightmare
of love, might rest her head on my shoulder,
stretch her legs, accept this once, my kiss on the neck.

After a Disappointing Visit with Old Friends, I Try in Vain to Recover the Joys of Childhood

Exhausted by excess, obsessions of our age
—the passage of time and eternal decay—
I take a walk through the crust of fallen snow:
just a dusting, so the grassless ground shows
through like scalp on a balding head. It's ugly,
but not shamelessly so. I by-pass the safety
of our small house for the smaller patch of timber
behind it. Here, after crossing the fallen wire
and four-post fence, I find, next to a tangle of
vines and thorns, old milkweed pods, snapped off
and stepped on, hollow and stiff. I rub the shells
in my palms and a few feathers drift down and fall.
I wish I could say they had a certain dignity.
My wife thinks I sulk too much. Truth is, I'm happy,
solitary, and if I close my eyes as I sit on the downed
oak log, I can almost hear the shouting children
who summers before scanned this ground for arrowheads,
for fossil prints on stone, for the mica shine
in beds of quartz. It didn't take much to please us.
Any oddity of surface became Geronimo's last arrow,
and we could make the dullest stone shine
with spit or with squinting against the sun.
So when I think the banal thought that time is loss,
that my modest home lacks the grace of past imaginings,
I can't forget the false but valued treasures
I once found breaking ground: the triangular rock

a friend unleashed missed my eye by inches.
We must be given happiness revising pleasure,
the patch of frosty pine we turn into a forest,
the simple fiction of the dig. I see it now, I feel it,
on my forehead, door to memory: an indentation, tiny star,
archeology of loss, the once-saved stone released.

III.

"Souls which recognise one another congregate together. Those which do not, argue with one another."

—Idries Shah
Caravan of Dreams

Zinfandel

Intense, peppery, spicy,
you won't last long.
You're like the woman
who gave me nightmares,
and who, thank God, I never met.
I watched her from a distance
bending over the plump red grapes,
dropping them in her basket
with a swipe of her sickle-shaped knife.
It looked like backbreaking work.
Possibly she enjoyed it. Possibly
she was forty and well-preserved,
though she looked twenty, her face
aged in sunlight. Her boy friend,
stubble-bearded gringo foreman,
sat on the cedar fence
making certain no one loafed.
I'm sure he was rarely sober
after noon, was routinely cruel
to children, dogs, to his aged mother
who brought his lunch in paper bags.
Until, perhaps, some cheap version
of vintage bourbon passed through his lips:
then sentiment ran wild, he became a confusion
of chatter and desire, running over women
with an array of kisses and promises.
Or so he claimed one August afternoon
when, half drunk, he took me on a tour
reserved for 'special friends.' It cost
twice as much. That's what I remember

about my journey to the Napa Valley
when I took my first drink
of exotic zinfandel. But the word alone
warmed me, seemed pure joy, an exclamation
of love in a foreign tongue. How unlike
the New England town where I now live,
where maple leaves turning red
prefigure fierce, disastrous winters.
I used to think of snow as harmless,
picturesque, until, trapped in a blizzard,
I almost froze to death in my old Ford.
Now, when storms break huge oak limbs
I wonder how anyone endures the winter.
So I'm obliged to that arid afternoon
when, in the town of Amador, I saw
my guide and his girl, face to face.
She wore a see-through blouse
and everybody stared. I wanted to cover her
as they swayed from the doorway to the bar,
exhausted, drunk, or both, to the curb
and back. He grabbed her arm, in love
I hope, and pulled her close.
He used a minimum of force
and she, in pleasure, winced. That's to say
I prefer to think them happy,
just as I prefer, to the imminent threat
of winter, to sip this tart red wine
whose tannin leaves a coating
on the tongue, an aftertaste,

an apparition, like that woman
and her transparent blouse, which I found
flimsy and romantic, unapproachable,
a useless kind of ecstasy.

Nazis

Thank God they're all gone
except for one or two in Clinton Maine
who come home from work
at Scott Paper or Diamond Match
to make a few crank calls
to the only Jew in New England
they can find

These make-shift students of history
whose catalogue of facts include
every Jew who gave a dollar
to elect the current governor
every Jew who'd sell this country out
to the insatiable Israeli state

I know exactly how they feel
when they say they want to smash my face

Someone's cheated them
they want to know who it is
they want to know who makes them beg
It's true Let's Be Fair
it's tough for almost everyone
I exaggerate the facts
to make a point

Just when I thought I could walk to the market
just when Jean the check-out girl
asks me how many cords of wood I chopped
and wishes me a Happy Easter
as if I've lived here all my life

Just when I can walk into the bank
and nod at the tellers who know my name
where I work who lived in my house in 1832
who know to the penny the amount
of my tiny Jewish bank account

Just when I'm sure we can all live together
and I can dine in their saltbox dining rooms
with the melancholy painting of Christ
on the wall their only consolation
just when I can borrow my neighbor's ladder
to repair one of the holes in my roof

I pick up the phone
and listen to my instructions

I see the town now from the right perspective
the gunner in the glass bubble
of his fighter plane shadowing the tiny man
with the shopping bag and pointy nose
his overcoat two sizes too large for him
skulking from one doorway to the next
trying to make his own way home

I can see he's not one of us

Checks and Balances: Oakland, Maine

for Ernie Pelotte

Though this town's falling down
invisibly, there's more to see
before escaping it. I suppose
I've traced this path a hundred times
but failed to notice how in June
the ripe white chestnut blooms
beside the overbearing skunkweed,
powders the air to fragrance
before falling as dust
on this very dusty road.

How unlike the Midwest,
where I'm going and where I've been,
cornfield after cornfield,
robin redbreast after banal blackbird,
without benefit of changing ocean breeze.

I suppose I can't wait to leave
and then come back, to visit the bigot
who "Jewed me down" on a cord of wood,
to pay homage to my asthmatic friend
who fixed the flashing on my roof.
Weeks later an ambulance picked him up
and packed him in, out of breath. In graceless
permanence. I saw them bolt the coffin,
drop him down. Now I'm closer to my death

each afternoon, after so many senseless moves
my shadow can't catch up. Could I embrace it,
could I climb the ladder that killed my friend,
could I have pulled the decaying leaves
from the overflowing gutter, I might have been
released from the commonplace, repeating breath.
But my neighbor left a piece of him,
a rusty nail on my roof, to ensure
that I'd be back in the fall. To watch
the leaves, brilliant reds and browns,
to watch a neighbor in need of firewood
bring his last healthy oak to the ground.

Ode to Experience

You make nothing possible.
You make the moon an elephant on its haunches.
Every love affair's another damaged visit
to my father and his strap. Every evening

your face is a desert, a tundra, your mouth is a tundra,
and I'm looking for you everywhere inside your clothes.
To reach you I eat dark bread, crawl inside the train.
I want your face filled in, a detailed map of the city.

I know why you made the suitcase so heavy.
I know why I can't think of your body
as a brother's. Why you're my closest neighbor.
Why I turn from the dark planets all night long.

You're with me in the morning: an eclipse.
Your kiss, the kiss of the ventriloquist.
Where else could I turn? I'm attached to you
the way the moon's married to evening. Before it rises.

Bleak House

for Dianne

Drunks in the courtyard, dung and driftwood
floating down the Thames, and some
poor swine sweats over his accounts.
The error's his. Standing on the bridge
in lamplight, the stars barricaded
by a wall of clouds, he knows
what chance he has. And the do-gooder
who pulls him down is also without a penny,
doomed to room in a pauper's grave.

Reader, this body's a shapeless mass,
made to fall apart. You don't want to hear
about the boy with so much promise,
who marries to improve himself. The old grouch
who gives away all his money
with a smile. Dear reader, the happy ending's
this: a little girl in curls
marries, gives herself up, is kept
to death and doesn't get a single kiss.
So wipe off that smirk. Your rich uncle's coming
to dinner, he's left you his precious disease.

Mahler

I forgive the Jew who wants to serve
the nailed-down Christ: who wouldn't want to rise
again, like morning, instead of mourning
all that's lost, falling on your knees in grief?
His drowned child was all descent, all guilt, all gone.

Each Sabbath before my poor father left,
we paraded past the service at the temple
to the baker, the cookie called meringue,
a sugar wafer melting on the tongue.
Its sweetness lasted in my mouth for hours.

The dust of angels is not made of flour.
Cannot be sifted. Will not rise. The door
is barred to Jews who love the shiny silk
before the flesh decays. Oh it's dark inside
the railroad cars, when the windows shake.

I too want to be saved. I too want to believe
in filling the open mouth with wine and wafer.
But we who lack fathers, sons, and holy ghosts,
the rag pickers in us, trip on the cobblestones.
All that flesh. A heavy cart to tug toward heaven.

Panorama

for Bibi Lee

I want the blossoms on the plum restored,
the palms that cloak the hummingbird,

but each time I blink my eye the shadow
of a redwood passes through me with a chill.

A young woman has been killed in the park
where my wife and I take our daily walks.

Each time our path twists through a breach
of pine, I think, *Here, they'll find her*

body here. I pursued the story in the papers,
as if grief were my daughter, as if the man

who struck her down struck down all possibility.
Yesterday, though, we hiked to a plateau

where the city of San Francisco, the whole
skyline abundant with afternoon light, shone.

Before this view, for the sake of Bibi Lee,
I hoped Keats was right, that pleasure could be

graded, like steps to eternity. Then living
while you're living might raise you to the clouds.

But we want the world. The world! I stood before it
like a man in a coffin while my wife held my hand.

I see that scene more clearly now than yesterday.
And I can almost sense the small bird's hum

dispatched from blossom to blossom, the sweetness
set against the lilac scent, the tarry smell

of wood, the herbaceous earth, the ripening plum
I still can't wait to eat.

Poem Against the
Invasion of Small Countries

I can't pretend to come to verdure honestly,
but I love the bacteria of my country:
the sound of cocci, bacilli, spirilla, without regard to source.
Those who guard the President's speech from spores

in the agar agar have never been given an orchid
by Orpheus, cannot possibly remember
the precise difficulty of genus and classification—
the mollusk as oyster, mussel, clam, or snail—

without considering a meal. They detest the face
of the eel because it's morbid and palpable.
If you should come upon the unsoiled mind, unspoiled
by governance and usage, please protect

its delegates. Those sea scrolls
we discover by the tidepools, luscious and obscure,
the muddy reds and browns, those not bound
by leaf, stem, or root. The ugly seaweed, pond scum,

paramecium, the original impurities—
like birthmarks on the water—
that make our lakes undrinkable and beautiful
to gaze at from a distance.

Notre Dame (1909)

after Francis Jammes

The padre's in a quandary, in sight of Notre Dame, God's grandeur built by working men. Its buttresses arch over the city like children's backs holding up the concrete burdens of the cross. From the bridge he watches warships in the harbor: they seem harmless in their idleness, but their sludge seeps invisibly into the sea.

Why is he disturbed? The landscape's unredeemed, intemperate clouds threaten rain. He almost likes the way a breeze puffs sails into waving handkerchiefs, the harbor in a reverie of adieus. But good-bye to what? To the debtors who sleep at the river's edge? He shakes them so they won't freeze; he knows there's no saving them.

Still, the padre's willful in his wish to be cheerful. After all, he's a friend of Dubuffet's. He's waved to him from the tower where the painter does his public service. No one knows exactly what he does. He also knows Apollinaire. They once sat beneath this very bridge, puffing on a single cigarette. While one professed his universal love, the other blushed. One stood up for the body, the other for the soul. They both agreed the city could be cruel and void of solitude, unlike the nearby countryside where Father tends his flock of fattened sheep.

As for the shifting clouds, the day seems made for questioning. Why's the Seine the same drained color of the sky? What goes on in all those cupolas? Whose windows darken with fear or love? The answer's in the future, in the quivering river, which, in a gust of wind, might sliver our reflections. There are wars to come, plagues of bombs to frighten even God. The padre wants no part of it, this shearing of the human. Then why is he so paralyzed? He can't stand still all day. The gendarme wants him off the bridge. The sight of him's discomfiting, like the child's lost balloon, hovering above the row houses, pensions, and small hotels. For the sky's where he belongs, looking down from the heights, first stranger of the century.

Honduras

The landing strip swarms with light.
From a distance: a teeming city, a marketplace.
But a cargo plane's come home from the dark,
from its dark deliveries. And its squealing brakes
don't sound like the squealing family pig
set out on a hook. Who knows how many citizens
are hidden in the trees? Their helmets, brown
and green, duplicate shade and sheath: banana leaf.

The pilot washes his face with his palms.
Takes inventory. The smoky cabin, dank
as a library, the dismembered charts, the bent-over
navigator, taking note of his slowing breath.
Each bomber has its accountant, its broken scholar.

The cross hairs of history make fine adjustments.
But in flight it's hard to see the burnt-out huts,
flooded paddies, the past's disguises, a few degrees
to the east, caught in laser light. Which is why
bright young men descend on the future, and land
in different continents than their fathers.

At the Jazz Concert

The sax shattered into eighth notes
as if it had been dropped.
I've only lived in America
for forty years, so I know the need
to invade, for kids to scream
at their mamas to stop slapping them
at the superette. The drummer's
taking out his history on the snare,
the trombones are terribly unstable,
and the whole cargo of notes could change
with a nod of the horn. The woman
who used to be your wife could start
a family on the struggling side of town.
Wouldn't it be nice to live in peace
in some far-off corner of the globe?
Now the bass is traveling:
we're resting at a truck stop
halfway between North Platte
and nowhere else. So tap your foot
to the national music. Your country's nightmare
is a mean café and you're effeminate.
The cowboy's gun is made to make you dance.

Mingus: Last Speech

For Eric Dolphy

When Eric left, we played
lost. Our septet faked his tunes
the way a soldier who'd lost a limb
might, in a rage, reach for it.

How he brought the phrase to peak
without talk. How he slaved
at parties, cornered with his sax,
played Bird's tunes to the phonograph.

He accompanied our dollar talk:
who did what gig, who paid what
and what for. At the end we fought—
different tunes in different heads.

No melodies in his. Or so I thought.
It was that clarinet I hate. Big, black,
ugly stick. It bellowed out. In leaps
and leaps. The tune could not keep up.

But that's exactly what I hear
in his music now, in his ear the bounds
of octaves broke, like the night
at Five Spot I croaked two strings

in our arranged "Mood Indigo."
Outside, windows broke, cops banged
tunes on brothers' heads. Paid off
per capita, the owner shrugged

and chased the man to Danish-land, where
he played over everyone's head. So sure
they'd appreciate it. "White devils," he
called them, but could not play back a hurt.

I made it for a while, though now
I'm crippled up. I should have heard him right.
If his music still does sing, he swings
high above it, at a price. Like fathers hung

in Birmingham thirty years before, he played
free songs off-base to a wrong audience. Twice.

Central Avenue Breakdown

The stars are out but the sky glows yellow and red with smelt clouds from the iron plants. The postwar depression's over, Truman says; our women are home, the idle days, the days of work by hand, are gone. Al Haber's borrowed thousands against his house to buy a small appliance store: the white porcelain washers and dryers, squat little robots, line up to save the modern housewife time. Time for what? No one knows just yet. Perhaps time to shop, to sleep, to ride through the countryside in the invincible Chevrolet.

Al's all confidence, leaning against the Elks Club wall in Watts; he wears his wide-brimmed hat and camel coat. Like the mustachioed man in the *Look* ad, he puffs on Lucky Strikes. He and his truck driver, Coffee; Coffee's gal, Lucille; and his cousin Ella have come to hear Wardell Gray and Dexter Gordon fight it out in the famous battle of the tenors. Coffee says, "I put my money on the Dex. No way a man that tall will lose his breath."

They play "Move," "Cottontail," "Scrapple from the Apple," and, in fiery counterpoint, "The Hunt." One instrument is plaintive, grievesome, high pitched: a little boy's whine. The other's cool, restrained, always in control. He can play all the changes, and, like the bragging boy genius, quote from everyone: Gershwin, Grofe, Prez, or Bird. They blow facing the audience, back to back, face to face, on their knees, while their pleated pants flap like signal flags to the drummer's beat. Their fans know how to read the signs. They know who sat in in Detroit, where they ate dinner the night before, who came and went, wrapped in furs, who was not alone when the lights went out.

"Truth's in the tonguing," Coffee says, and the two couples laugh. "That's how they get the tone."

The tone moves from reverence to delirium, from whispers to shouts. "Play that thing," "Take it, take it," and "Uh-huh," punctuate each solo riff. It's the Gospel Meeting of the Saxophone. Blacks and whites stand shoulder to shoulder, snapping fingers, clapping hands. If Al's white paw on Ella's thigh turns some heads in the smoky light of the crowded club, the looks are easy to ignore. "Don't mind them," Lucille tells Al, "even Dex has his own vanilla bean."

"Then here's to the future," Al says, lifting his glass of Scotch. "May it include us all."

"It's our funeral," Coffee says, downing his whiskey. He can't stand the thought of the future, the day after the day after, when today's bills must be paid.

"Don't be that way," Coffee's cousin Ella says "You'll upset my man." Ella takes good care of Al: she makes sure his drink's refilled, she dresses in the clothes he likes, she keeps him interested. Al's left his wife at home: she likes Mozart and Bizet, the smell of baked goods in the oven. A driveway and a flower garden. When Coffee came to pick Al up, she was reading on their terrace and barely said hello.

"I bet she's been to England," Coffee said.

"Ah nerts," was Al's retort. "She's from Philly, just like me. She's just been to school."

In nineteen forty-seven, in the blooming shadows of the Elks Club, everybody goes to school. Young musicians behind the stand take notes with their feet. They nod when the rhythm section punctuates the proper sentence. Sometimes they almost swoon. There's Eric Dolphy, the skinny, shy home-town boy with the bump on his head. "My extra brain," he says. There's Sonny Criss. There's the Texan, Ornette Coleman, who likes to hear tunes differently. He likes to hear them wrong. He's sure that's how the future hears them.

Al goes to school with his ears. He learns the language that frightened his family back to the hills: the hipsters' hoot and drawl: "zoot suit," "tom cat," "groovin' high." Not the pallid "swell" or "gosh," not the mannered white boys' talk.

In the second set the tenors plummet darker, into "Lover Man," "Old Folks," and "Body and Soul." Al's never heard these tunes turned so deep in reverie, the melodies awry. The sudden violent honks make him feel as if he's rubbed his forehead on a stucco wall. "They shouldn't play that way," he says, gesturing for the waiter to bring him another Scotch. "My head's all scratched."

"They can't help the way they play," Ella says. "But I can make it better. Put down that worry juice," she adds, takes his free hand and slips it down her blouse. Then she strokes his sweaty forehead with her palm, while Coffee looks at them and laughs.

"You've got it all, my ofay friend," he says. "No money down, infinity to pay."

"Don't be that way," Ella repeats her plea, like a refrain, a chorus of the blues.

Al stares wholly into the bell of the saxophone, the dark spiral, the little cornucopia, the open mouth, the twisted tunnel leading who knows where? The next thing he knows there's a Negro soldier who's going to Korea, who's had too much to drink, too little to touch. He hisses out a name, a mean remark: the words ripple outward, opening the space around him. There's a tiny rumble almost no one notices. Al's silk tie soaks up the blood on his lip. Someone gives him an ice cube, while his head spins for an explanation. He doesn't even know the man. Now what can he tell his white wife? She'd know where he'd been; she'd know, as Lucille'd say, "Somethin's been cookin' in her oven." But later, when he slides back into his own bed and his wife barely wakes to take his hand, she won't ask him anything. She lets him sidle up in their favorite spoon. In a minute they'll both be sleeping, and Al will dismiss the night as history: he'll forget the slap. The pain. The nameless crime.

But sometime later he'll wake to the gray and flaking ash of the future: clouds hovering over a city like the A-bomb dropped on foreign soil. The future's blank. Arrives in a big black Olds, a hearse car, a "battleship on wheels." Arrives with a TV set he sits before all day, a set where someone's naming names, where someone stands accused. But who? Al won't go out, won't step foot in Coffee's neighborhood. Someone's out there, in here, over there, like the communists. The cleaning lady can't get rid of them, even Ike can't get rid of them. They're the knife point and gun belt, the lighter in the alley, the dark desire in every utterance. They're the insect on the psychotic's robe, they're the slamming of the bedroom door. He knew they'd be coming. Coming to get him. To take away everything that's his.

What he didn't know was this: Dexter lost his cabaret card, courtesy of no one knows; his white girl won't bail him out of jail. Someone steals his instrument: later he'll play in Paris, Copenhagen: we'll be his exile. In the meantime, in the cell he stoops over, he grows old and small, almost invisible. Like Wardell, who they found slumped over the steering wheel of a Ford in the desert. The desert where bombs are tested. It was over a girl, Al heard. Over the mob. Over drugs. It was over.

Al does not become fat or thin. His business thrives and dies, is bought out and lives again. He sits in the safety of his living room, listens to Miles play "Easy Livin'," on his record machine. He closes his eyes. There, in the melancholy melody, are the black faces he's forgotten. There's Coffee—who he's fired and fired again—there's the friend of a friend, there's the dark woman with her darker tongue: she's kissing him, erasing his body with her lips. First the neck is gone, then the cheeks, then the ears and eyes, the fluid in the skull, the genitals. He's lost his body there, in the echo of the saxophone, in the melody of memory, in the swelling and shrinking heart. And there's nowhere to turn from it, from those he's already turned from. He's the stunned blank face to be filled in, the brick thrown through the store window, the paper that lights the storefront, the scrawled graffiti on the walls that call his name.

North Platte: August, 1968

We were numb to Nebraska,
stunned by a land so austere
we feared the Sioux would not survive
the monotone of country road.

Though in love, we did not include
in our romance the constancy
of cornfields, the slackened flags
above each roadside stand. We lived inside

a grand idea: we could change The State.
I remember stripping down
in that cheap hotel
while the woman who'd become my wife

lay naked on the bed. Cranky,
weary beyond reason, we made love
to prove love possible.
Then we turned the TV on

to watch the mayor of Chicago
turn loose his crew of cops with clubs.
It could have been Haymarket, Peekskill,
until I saw a face like mine,

young and bearded, bloody up the screen.
Then we became static, a little buzz
in history. It was for me
the end of politics. Oh we marched,

we marched the way we always march:
a step behind a caravan of trucks
that dragged its sheep and cows
to a yard behind the railroad tracks.

At the Half Note Café

for Gene Ammons

Once I heard him play
"Willow Weep for Me"
in a tone so full
and sentimental, I felt
a gap between my ribs
and lungs, a dearth of air
sorrow soon enough would fill.
I found the blues unfair
to boys like me who came to bars
unprepared for grief
that wasn't strictly personal.

I told my girl
I knew all you had to know
about suffering and love, but when
I heard a woman drunk, cry out,
in front of everyone, "Don't go, Jug—
I'll give you all of what you want,"
my face went blank
and limp as an infant
when a stranger shakes
a rattle in his face. Later,
when he hit bottom,
the last broken chorus
of "Body and Soul," I collapsed in
my girl's arms, my composure crushed
by one note on the saxophone.
I couldn't think of what to tell her.
What the hell did she know anyhow?
We both came from the same suburban town.

It was a brittle winter night.
We had nowhere to go
except her parents' house,
so we drifted down Greenwich Ave.
hand in hand. I'd never seen
streets so crowded after dark—
with drunks, half-dead, and kids
who should have been in bed.
I'm shocked we made it out alive.
I know if I'd seen my stupid grin,
my wide-eyed stare, my gaping face,
I would have smashed it
just for the experience. We were lucky
though we didn't know it then. We ended up
parking in my mother's car. We kissed,
then I stripped off her blouse,
grabbed her breast,
put her stiffened nipple in my mouth.

Civil Rights

Biloxi, Freedom Summer, 1964

Mississippi steamed in July,
but who expected palm trees
to shade the colonials, so elegant
I could not afford to dream there?
Every day it almost rained. I slept
in railroad cars and cardboard shacks.
Black families fed me sides of pork.

The New York suburbs brought me there.
A Jewish boy with time to spare,
my guilt grew far from Mississippi.

I picketed the Dixie Country Store.
While customers turned white with spit
at the leaflet in my hand, my hand
that quivered, paper thin,
one cop in a helmet—just one cop—
bashed my fingers, turning them to claws.

I think I liked the sight of blood.
I got my dreamy night in jail,
a decent meal, a toilet and a bed.
I curled against the cooling walls
of cinder block and listened to
the ocean break the waves to mist.

Now I'm thinking of the ruts
the dirt roads cleaned by rake,
where, that July, I kicked up dust
before I rode the bus back home
to breathe the birches and the pines.
I thought my heart was wood.
In my neighborhood private cops
patroled at night to help us sleep.

Brief Afternoons

In the brief afternoons of February,
when the whole God question comes up
like a knock on the door from Jehovah's witnesses—
no, not *like* them, but *really* them
and their stack of newspapers and questions, swirling
in the snow—I'm cautious, impatient, defenseless.
I guard the door like St. Peter or Cerberus,
The Word before it's written. We discuss the proof
of the snowflake, God's design and the sin of the self.
We require uplifting because of the chill
and the solitude, because we project onto the pines
endings and beginnings, the whiteness of snow
in the darkening quill of afternoon,
where January can no longer be corrected; December's
a parent's perpetual death and July a child's fairy tale.
But now they're at my door with their gloomy accusations,
and because of the lateness of the hour,
because I have no defense, no justification
outside myself, I invite them in for hot chocolate—
together, white man and black man, the lapsed
and the saved, we watch the wind push the snow,
we listen to the woodstove chatter and whisper and hiss.

Emotional Traffic

was set in Sabon, a typeface designed by Jan Tschichold. The roman is based on a font engraved by Garamond and the italic on a font by Granjon, but Tschichold introduced many refinements to make these models suitable for contemporary typographic needs. Typeset by DEKR Corporation, Woburn, Massachusetts. Printed and bound by Maple-Vail Book Manufacturing Group, Binghamton, New York.